ThE SAFE TOUCh BOOK

Written by Dr. Beth Robinson
Illustrated by Noel Green

To respond to the message of this book,
for more information about Beth's speaking,
and for details on how to order additional copies of
The Safe Touch Book, please contact her at

Dr. Beth Robinson
P.O. Box 100
New Deal, TX 79350

Email: Beth.Robinson.@LCU.EDU
World Wide Web: DrBethRobinson.com

ISBN-13: 978-0-9799092-2-1

Printed in the United States of America

The world is filled with wonderful things.
There are the sun, the moon, and the stars.
There are plants and animals.
And the most wonderful thing of all is me.

I have a wonderful body.
I have arms and legs so I can play.
I have eyes and ears and a nose.
Every year, my body grows and changes.

I have a wonderful body and I need to take care of it.
I need to brush my teeth, wash my hands,
and keep my body safe.

I need to keep my body safe.
I don't need to allow other people to hit me, to push me,
or to touch me in a way that makes me feel bad.
This is one way I can keep my body safe.

Touches that make me feel bad are not safe touches.
When someone pushes me or hits me or
touches me in a way that makes me feel bad,
I need to shout "Stop!" and tell a grownup.

Some touches make me feel good.
These touches are safe touches.
Safe touches can be a hug from my mom or dad
or holding hands with a friend.

My body has special private parts.
My private parts are the parts I cover
with a swimsuit when I go swimming.

When I was a baby, my parents touched
my private parts when they changed my diaper.
They had to clean my private parts when I was a baby.

Now that I am bigger, a doctor or nurse may examine
my private parts in a doctor's office.
They do this to help my body stay healthy.

But if anyone else wants to touch my private parts,
I will say "No!" and tell a grownup I trust.

People I can trust are grownups who help keep me safe
and who won't let other people hurt me.

If someone tells me they will hurt me if I tell,
I need to tell a grownup I trust about the touches.
The only way I can be safe and the people I love can be safe
is for me to tell a grownup I trust about the touches.

Keeping me safe is the job of the grownups.
My job is to tell if anyone hits me
or touches me in an unsafe way.
When I tell a grownup I trust, I won't get in trouble.

If someone wants me to look at
or touch their private parts,
I will say "No!" and tell a grownup I trust.

If someone tries to touch my private parts,
I will keep telling grownups that I trust
until someone believes me and makes the touching stop.

I have a wonderful body and
I need to do what I can to keep my body safe.

JUST FOR PARENTS

The Safe Touch Book is designed to help prevent sexual abuse from occurring. If you are like many other parents, you don't know how to begin to talk to your children about sexual abuse. Hopefully, this book will provide an easy way for you to open up conversations about sexual safety. You can read *The Safe Touch Book* to your children multiple times. Through repeated reading of the book, your children will learn to tell you if adults or other children are touching them inappropriately. In addition, you and your child will begin to talk about sexuality in a nonthreatening way that will make it easier for you to answer questions as your child gets older.

If your child discloses that he or she has been touched inappropriately or sexually abused, you need to contact your local law enforcement or children's protective services. If you have additional questions about how to use this coloring book, you may contact Dr. Robinson through her website: DrBethRobinson.com

Additional resources about child sexual abuse may be found by contacting the following organizations.

National Council on Child Abuse and Family Violence

This nonreligious organization provides intergenerational violence prevention services by bringing together community and national professionals and volunteers to prevent domestic violence, child abuse, and elder abuse.

Phone: (202) 429-6695
Website: NCCAFV.org

Childhelp

Childhelp® is a leading national nonprofit organization dedicated to helping victims of child abuse and neglect. Childhelp's approach focuses on prevention, intervention, and treatment. The Childhelp National Child Abuse Hotline operates 24 hours a day, seven days a week.

Phone: (800) 4-A-CHILD
Website: ChildHelp.org

Also Available from Dr. Beth Robinson

The Safe Touch Coloring Book

God Made Me: A Safe Touch Coloring Book

The Safe Family Coloring Book

When A Friend Dies

Where Will I Grow Up

CPSIA information can be obtained at www.ICGtesting.com
Printed in the USA
LVOW02s1223020614

388203LV00008B/20/P